Where's the water?

WATER CONSERVATION

By Peter Castellano

Gareth Stevens
PUBLISHING

Please visit our website, www.garethstevens.com. For a free color catalog of all our high-quality books, call toll free 1-800-542-2595 or fax 1-877-542-2596.

Library of Congress Cataloging-in-Publication Data

Names: Castellano, Peter, author.
Title: Water conservation / Peter Castellano.
Description: New York : Gareth Stevens Publishing, [2017] | Series: Where's
   the water? | Includes bibliographical references and index.
Identifiers: LCCN 2016011906 | ISBN 9781482446920 (pbk.) | ISBN 9781482446944 (library bound) | ISBN
9781482446937 (6 pack)
Subjects: LCSH: Water conservation–Juvenile literature. |
   Water–Pollution–Juvenile literature. | Water-supply–Juvenile literature.
Classification: LCC TD388 .C37 2017 | DDC 333.91/16–dc23
LC record available at http://lccn.loc.gov/2016011906

First Edition

Published in 2017 by
Gareth Stevens Publishing
111 East 14th Street, Suite 349
New York, NY 10003

Designer: Katelyn E. Reynolds
Editor: Kristen Nelson

Photo credits: Cover, p. 1 Thomas Barrat/Shutterstock.com; cover, pp. 1–24 (background) vitalez/
Shutterstock.com; pp. 4–21 (circle splash) StudioSmart/Shutterstock.com; p. 5 Tania Kolinko/
Shutterstock.com; p. 7 nomadFra/Shutterstock.com; p. 9 Tanmoy Bhaduri/Pacific Press/LightRocket
via Getty Images; p. 11 haveseen/Shutterstock.com; p. 13 Kekyalyaynen/Shutterstock.com;
p. 15 (main) NASA/JPL; p. 15 (inset) NASA/JPL-Caltech/University of California, Irvine; p. 17
BAY ISMOYO/AFP/Getty Images; p. 19 Zekeriya Gunes/Anadolu Agency/Getty Images; p. 20
Patricia Hofmeester/Shutterstock.com.

CONTENTS

Words in the glossary appear in **bold** type the first time they are used in the text.

WE NEED WATER!

Water is important for all life on Earth. However, it's a nonrenewable **resource**, which means there's only a limited amount of it. In fact, the amount of water on Earth has been about the same for millions of years. The human population has grown, though, and the need for clean water is higher than ever.

Population growth, along with pollution and global **climate change**, is greatly affecting the water on Earth. That's why conserving, or caring for, Earth's water is very important.

facts on Tap

Water covers more than 70 percent of our planet's surface. Only about 2.5 percent of

We need clean water to drink, cook, and wash. What would you do without it?

5

POLLUTION

Water pollution happens in many ways. After it rains or snows, water makes its way back into lakes and rivers carrying dirt and trash from our streets and yards. It may carry **chemicals** used on farms or in factories. This water is called runoff, and it can further contaminate, or pollute, waterways.

Groundwater, or the water naturally stored underground, can also be polluted by mining waste. As mining occurs, matter and chemicals that may be harmful to people and animals can enter the water supply.

Facts on Tap

Runoff can carry animal and human waste into waterways, too. People can get very sick if they drink water contaminated with waste.

Trash pollution in the ocean is a real problem. Big patches of trash, mostly plastic, float in oceans all over the world. Ocean animals may eat it or become tangled in it and drown.

GETTING WARMER

Other pollution affects our water as well. The burning of **fossil fuels** has played a part in climate change. And climate change is a big reason we must work on conserving water all over the world.

Climate change is causing some bodies of water to dry up. It's also causing glaciers to melt, making oceans less salty and perhaps harming the animals and plants living in them. Climate change is affecting all sorts of water **habitats**, possibly causing animals to have too little food or to have to find new homes.

Facts on Tap

Global climate change is causing Earth's weather to become more

As glaciers melt, water levels are rising in Earth's oceans. Ghoramara Island, off the east coast of India, has lost about 50 percent of its land to rising ocean water!

9

A DRY TIME

A drought is a period of time when an area has much less **precipitation** than usual. Local governments often have to make rules about how and when water is used so there isn't a shortage.

Many times, conservation efforts during a drought include using groundwater. But since there's no precipitation to replace the groundwater being used, too much of this important resource may be used in some areas. Scientists say this will cause even more problems in the future as parts of Earth get drier.

Facts on Tap

Hundreds of gallons of water a year can be wasted by leaky sinks and showers. Tell your parents to get them fixed. They can save money and water!

Water conservation efforts are important during a drought. California has had drought conditions for years. Some people promised not to wash their cars for a couple of months in order to conserve water!

WASTEWATER

Wastewater is any water that's been used, such as the water that goes down the drain when you take a shower. One major water conservation effort is cleaning that water at a treatment plant. Then, it can be used again.

However, water treatment plants may not be able to remove all pollutants from water, such as some kinds of soap, which could harm the **environment**. Sometimes the level of chemicals in water can be too much for the treatment plant to handle and can make people sick.

Wastewater treatment plants, like this one, allow us to reuse wastewater. Keeping an eye on water **quality** is very important at these plants.

13

GRACE

NASA (National Aeronautics and Space Administration) is partly using its GRACE **mission** to check Earth's groundwater levels from space. GRACE uses **satellites**, spacecraft, and measurements from scientists on Earth to find how the amount of freshwater on Earth is changing.

The GRACE mission has been used to watch the long drought in California. It showed that between 2003 and 2010 the groundwater in the Central Valley of California had gone down enough to cause concern. The groundwater hasn't returned to earlier, higher levels since.

Facts on Tap

GRACE began in 2002. Its findings have also shown scientists how ice sheets, glaciers, and oceans are changing.

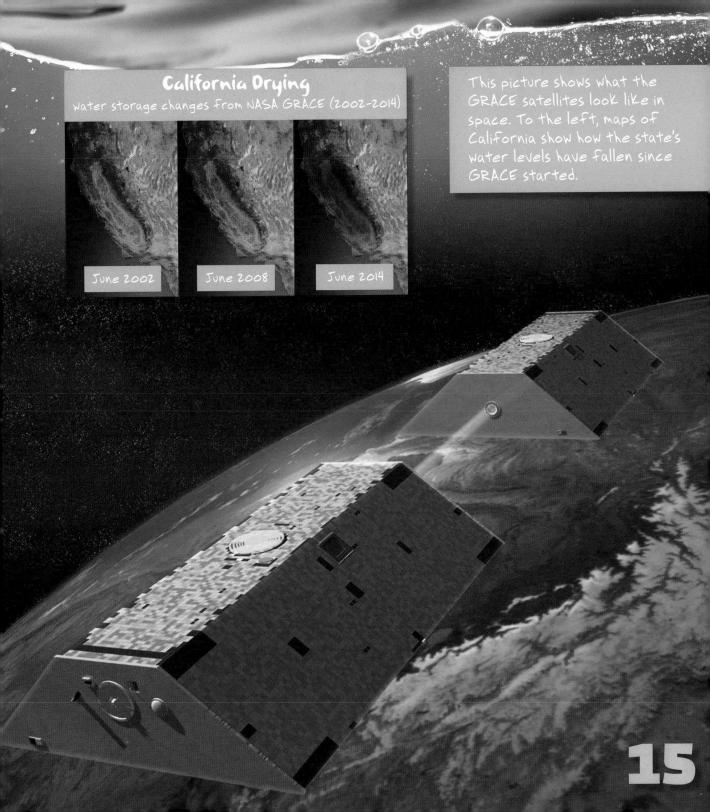

California Drying
water storage changes from NASA GRACE (2002-2014)

June 2002

June 2008

June 2014

This picture shows what the GRACE satellites look like in space. To the left, maps of California show how the state's water levels have fallen since GRACE started.

15

WATER LAWS

In 1948, the US government passed the first major law to address water pollution. Since then, many other laws have been passed to keep drinking water safe and plentiful.

But there's still a lot to be done in the United States to better conserve water. The pipes of some water systems in the country date back to the 1800s! They leak and may allow harmful matter into drinking water. However, fixing these pipes could cost the government trillions of dollars!

Facts on Tap

Starting in 1994, the US government required companies to make low-flow showerheads, sinks, and toilets. Today, these are commonly found in homes and businesses.

On March 22 of every year, we celebrate World Water Day. Each year highlights a topic about making clean water an important project around the world.

CLEAN WATER FOR ALL

More than 7.3 billion people live on Earth. It's been reported that by 2025, about 1.8 billion people will live in an area that doesn't have enough water. What's more, some places don't have any way to clean the water they do have.

Groups like World Vision have been working for many years toward all people having clean water. They've helped more than 2 million people in Africa by digging wells there and teaching people how to

Some places don't have bathroom water separate from their drinking water, which can make people sick. Building wells and teaching people about **sanitation** can save many lives.

19

DO YOUR PART!

Conserving water is important—and you can help!

Meat and dairy products take a lot of water to produce because they come from animals that need water to live. Eating fewer meat and dairy products can help save water. So can simply taking a shower instead of a bath or shortening your shower by just a couple of minutes!

Could you turn off the water when you brush your teeth? Or collect rainwater to water your garden? Small efforts are a big help in water conservation on Earth!

By conserving water, you're helping your family save money, too.

How Much Water?

to flush a toilet:
as much as 3.5 gallons (13 L)

to fill a bathtub:
70 gallons (265 L)

to fill a pool:
22,000 gallons (83,280 L)

to grow and process
a pound of cotton:
100 gallons (379 L)

to produce one glass
of milk:
54 gallons (204 L)

to fly cross-country:
almost 6,000 gallons (22,712 L)

GLOSSARY

chemical: matter that can be mixed with other matter to cause changes

climate change: long-term change in Earth's climate, caused partly by human activities such as burning oil and natural gas

environment: the natural world in which a plant or animal lives

extreme: great or severe

fossil fuel: matter formed over millions of years from plant and animal remains that is burned for power

habitat: the natural place where an animal or plant lives

mission: a task or job a group must perform

precipitation: rain, snow, sleet, or hail

quality: the standard or grade of something

resource: a usable supply of something

sanitation: the act or process of making something clean and free from factors that could harm health

satellite: an object that circles Earth in order to collect and send

FOR MORE INFORMATION

Books

Kallen, Stuart A. *Running Dry: The Global Water Crisis*. Minneapolis, MN: Twenty-First Century Books, 2015.

Rake, Jody Sullivan. *Endangered Oceans: Investigating Oceans in Crisis*. North Mankato, MN: Capstone Press, 2015.

Websites

The Water Cycle for Schools
water.usgs.gov/edu/watercycle-kids.html
Investigate the water cycle to learn more about water on Earth.

WaterSense Kids
epa.gov/watersense/kids/
Find out some simple ways to save water on the EPA's website for kids.

Water Use It Wisely
wateruseitwisely.com/kids/
Play games and learn many ways you can take part in water conservation.

INDEX